Graceful, Gliding Gulls;
A Kids Picture Book With Fun Facts About Seagulls

Faye Elliott

Copyright and Disclaimers

Graceful, Gliding Gulls; A Kids Picture Book With Fun Facts About Seagulls
By Faye Elliott
Copyright © 2013, All Rights Reserved. Except for the use in any review. The reproduction or utilization of this work in whole or in part in any form by any electronic, mechanical or other means is forbidden without permission of the author.

Published By:

NC Beach Photography
Newport, NC 28570
NcBeachPhoto.com

Legal Disclaimer:

The author and publisher have made every effort to supply accurate and thorough information in the creation of this report. But, they offer no warranty and accept no responsibility for any loss or damages of any kind that may be incurred by the reader as a result of actions arising from the use of information found in this report.

The author and publisher reserve the right to make any changes they deem necessary to future versions of the publication to ensure its accuracy.

The reader assumes all responsibility for the use of the information within this report.

Table of Contents

Gliding & Soaring

Have you ever watched a seagull as it soars through the air? They are very graceful and believe it or not, they have a very fascinating life full of adventure, danger and mischief.

Different Gulls

Some people believe that if you've seen one gull,
you've seen them all, but that's not true. There are over
40 different species of gulls in the world.

Each has different markings, but all gulls have long curved wings and a strong beak.

Webbed Feet

Gulls also have webbed feet which makes them an excellent swimmer.

Waterproof

Did you know that the seagull's feathers are waterproof? There is a very thin coating of oil on each feather that prevents the water from soaking in. The oil comes from a gland at the base of the tail and the gull uses its bill to spread the oil all over its feathers.

That's why they always look so well-groomed even
after they've snatched a fish out of the water.

Master Thieves

Some Gulls are master thieves. They will steal the food right out of another gulls mouth. If that doesn't work, they will badger the victim until the bird drops its catch.

Laughing Gull

Sometimes the laughing gull will hitch a ride on the back of a pelican and wait for just the right moment to snatch the food from its bill.

Then they will fly away making a laughing noise.

What Seagulls Eat

Gulls are not fussy eaters. They will eat anything –
seeds, insects, worms, mice, dead animals, and even
garbage. Seafood is one of their favorite dishes,

Cracking Open Shells

especially shellfish, and they are even willing to work
for it. In order to get inside a clam or oyster shell, the
gull must take it high up and drop it on the concrete to
break it open. Sometimes they must do it over and over

again to get it to crack. If you ever go near the shore, you will see cracked shells all over the parking lot and walkways.

Following Fishing Boats

Flocks of seagulls will also glide behind a fishing boat waiting for bits of food. If a fisherman throws out a fish, a seagull will catch it in the air.

Flying Low

When a seagull flies slowly and gracefully over the water, he is looking for dead or wounded fish floating on the surface. When spotted, he drops to the water and snatches it up.

Seagull Calls

All gull calls are important to breeding, mating,
signaling alarm and warning, calling for attack, hunger,
assembly and begging. The young cry for food, or
scream while exercising their wings.

There are a wide range of sounds – sometimes they might sound like sheep, cats, puppies or hens. Sometimes when a gull begins a call, it will trigger others to join in and it sounds like a loud singing chorus of cheers.

Seagull Games

Life is not all work and no play for gulls. They like to play a friendly game of tag. One gull catches a fish and flies past others teasing them. Right away the chase is on! The first gull to catch the bait is it, and the fun continues until they are all to tired to play any more. At this point, the fish is dropped.

Valuable Gulls

Most people enjoy watching gulls and feeding them at
the beach. Gulls are so valuable to us in America that
they are protected by law. They are constantly at work,
cleaning up our beaches, harbors and garbage dumps.
They also help farmers by gobbling up insects that
destroy crops.

Gulls are one of the most adaptable birds in the world, and should be congratulated for learning to profit from our wasteful ways!

Bibliography

Animals of the Seashore – Julie Becker Copyright
EMC Corp. 1977, 1982 Page 47

Nature's Children – Grolier 1986 by Grolier Limited –
Pages 5, 6, 14, 18, 21

Watching Water Birds – Jim Arnosky- National
Geographic Society Copyright 1997

All Photo's were taken by my husband Dave Hashley -
N.C Beach Photography **NcBeachPhoto.com**

Printed in Great Britain
by Amazon

33738403R00016